The Safe Place

Patricia St. John

Illustrated by
Jeff Anderson

Published 2003 by Christian Focus Publications
Reprinted 2005
ISBN 1-85792-779-6
Text copyright © 2003 Patricia St. John
Ilustration copyright © 2003 Jeff Anderson
This edition copyright © 2003 Christian Focus Publications
www.christianfocus.com

This book was given to

....

with love from

....

"Jesus died to save," Romans 5:6-9.

The farm lay blazing in the midsummer heat; the harvest was in and the corn stacked, and it would soon be time for fruit picking.

The farmer leaned on the gate and gazed at the stubble fields. It had been a good crop, and he had done well on the poultry too.

Bill, the farm-hand was also having a rest under the haystack. He had finished his lunch and his mug of ale and was smoking a cigarette. There was half an hour to go, and it was pleasant in the shade of the rick. A warm smell of herbs came from the farm garden; it made Bill feel drowsy... he closed his eyes. Bill was asleep.

He woke suddenly, only a few minutes later, and wondered where the loud crackling noise came from. Then he smelt the smoke and leaped to his feet with a cry of horror.

The cigarette stump had rolled into the burnt grass, but it had done its deadly work. Already the rick was ablaze and the flames blowing toward the hen-coops and the house. Bill ran as he had never run before. The farmer would be at his dinner and they must phone the fire brigade.

Nothing could be done about the rick. It had already turned from a smouldering heap to a leaping furnace of flame: but they might save the poultry and the house.

He burst into the house like a madman, picked up the phone and dialed the fire department.

"Come quick," he urged. "It's on the main road - two and a half miles out."

He flung down the receiver, and found the farmer, pale-faced at his elbow.

"The barn's caught," he told Bill shortly, "so now it's the poultry and the house. Open the three gates into the meadow and shoo all the poultry towards them - they'll find their way; and I'll get the hose onto the coops and the wall of the house."

Together they fought the flames till their faces were black and their eyebrows singed. The farmer's wife had taken the children to the far end of the paddock and was hurriedly carrying out their most precious possessions in armfuls. She was the first to hear the clanging of the fire bell and to see the engine sweep into the yard.

It took some time to get the flames under control. The rick and the barn burned down into a sodden mass of ashes, but the hencoops, the house and the stable were saved.

The wife carried the most precious possessions back into the house, and made cups of tea for the weary firemen. Bill slunk off home before anyone got round to asking how the fire started.

The farmer went out to the coops and put down the chicken feed, and the poultry came wandering back, squawking and suspicious. He counted them carefully; one family was missing, the little white hen and her chickens.

The farmer looked towards the barn. "Where could they have got to?" he wondered. The chickens were very young - nine little fluffy balls of yellow down. But he had seen them running after the hen towards the safety of the open field, and she was an excellent mother. He would go and have a look around.

There were three openings in the stone wall leading out to the fields and the farmer went out at the main gate and walked slowly, examining the ditches. Finding nothing, he made for the small stile nearest the blazing barn, and here he stopped short, and stood staring at the ground. The hen sat in a heap in the gap, her head hanging over on one side, her feathers scorched and discoloured by smoke. She was quite dead, and yet the path to safety lay in front of her and the way was open. Why had she sat down and died like that?

The farmer stooped and picked her up, and out from under her limp wings ran the nine fluffy chickens, alive and cheeping. The farmer gathered them into a box and put them by the kitchen stove cuddled up in a piece of blanket. The seven-year-old just could not get over it.

"She could easily have saved herself, couldn't she, Daddy?" she kept saying, "but I suppose they were too small to run fast. Perhaps they couldn't see the way in the smoke? Perhaps they were going the wrong way? Anyhow, she knew the safest place was under her wings, didn't she, Daddy? I suppose she just sat down and called them to come, and died instead of them. Wasn't she a good mother, Daddy!"

However, the farmer's wife wasn't very happy. "I shan't have much time to be a good mother if I've got to bring that lot up by hand," she grumbled. "As though I hadn't enough to do already!"

But the seven-year-old laid her curly head against the blanket and whispered, "The gate was open. The hen could have saved herself; but she might have left her little ones behind, lost in the smoke. Little chickens, little chickens, I'm so glad you came when your mummy called you, or you'd all be dead. Little chickens, I'll be your mummy instead."

Talk About This

Who died to save us?

Jesus died to save us from eternal death. Jesus was sinless. He could have gone back to heaven without dying; but He would have gone alone. We would have remained cut off from God because of our sins, and to be separated from God finally leads to real, eternal death. So Jesus chose to die instead of us, so that He can now call us to come to Him and live.

What The Bible Says

When we were still without strength ... Christ died for the ungodly. For scarcely for a righteous man will one die; yet perhaps for a good man someone would dare to die. But God demonstrates His love to us, in that while we were still sinners Christ died for us. Much more then, having been justified by His blood, we shall be saved from wrath through Him," Romans 5:6-9.

"This is how we know what love is: Christ gave His life for us," 1 John 3:16.

"I live by faith in the Son of God who loved me and gave His life for me," Galatians 2:20.

"For God so loved the world that He gave His only begotten Son that whosoever believes in Him should not perish but have everlasting life," John 3:16.

What Jesus Said
"O Jerusalem, Jerusalem, the one who kills the prophets and stones those who are sent to her! How often I wanted to gather your children together, as a hen gathers her chicks under her wings, but you were not willing," Matthew 23:37.

Prayer: Lord, I understand that you loved me enough to die for me, that I might have eternal life, and you will call me to come and shelter in Jesus from sin and eternal death. Teach me to answer your call. Thank you for loving me; thank you for dying for me.

Think: Jesus allowed others to torture him to death for our sake. Can his love still be doubted? Do you think this can help you to bear suffering for others?

Other Scripture passages to read:

How Jesus gave his life to save sinners
Matthew Chapter 27, Mark Chapter 15
Luke Chapters 22-23, John Chapter 19

Jesus' Resurrection
Matthew Chapter 28, Mark Chapter 16
Luke Chapter 24, John Chapter 20.

CHRISTIAN FOCUS
Good Books with the Real Message of Hope